For Alexis (and his wonderful folks)! – T.M.
To Emily, Matilda and Jacob, with love x – H.S.

OXFORD
UNIVERSITY PRESS

Great Clarendon Street, Oxford OX2 6DP
Oxford University Press is a department of the University of Oxford.
It furthers the University's objective of excellence in research, scholarship,
and education by publishing worldwide. Oxford is a registered trade mark of
Oxford University Press in the UK and in certain other countries

Copyright © Tom Moorhouse 2017
Illustrations © Holly Swain 2017

The moral rights of the author and illustrator have been asserted
Database right Oxford University Press (maker)

First published 2017

British Library Cataloguing in Publication Data
Data available

ISBN: 978-0-19-274675-7

1 3 5 7 9 10 8 6 4 2

Printed in China

Paper used in the production of this book is a natural,
recyclable product made from wood grown in sustainable forests.
The manufacturing process conforms to the environmental
regulations of the country of origin.

Photographs: p154 (top) © Peter Turner Photography/Shutterstock, p154
(bottom) © Ermi/Shutterstock, p156 © Val Payne/Shutterstock.

THE NEW ADVENTURES OF MR TOAD

Toad Hall in Lockdown

Tom Moorhouse
with pictures by **Holly Swain**

OXFORD
UNIVERSITY PRESS

Contents

A Recent History of Toad Hall   6

Chapter 1
Turbo-boost   11

Chapter 2
Battle of the Hoovers   19

Chapter 3
Down the Hatch   31

Chapter 4
Modern Marvels   39

Chapter 5
Safe as Houses   47

Chapter 6
Squirrel Stakeout   57

Chapter 7
Sale of the Century   67

Chapter 8
The TechnoToad KG 1908   79

Chapter 9
Toad Hall Lockdown   89

Chapter 10
Always Read the Small Print   99

Chapter 11
Eggs of Vengeance   109

Chapter 12
Look what You've Done to Toad Hall   119

Chapter 13
The Coming of Wildwood's Uppance   123

Chapter 14
Toad Foolery   131

Chapter 15
Underground Insecurity   139

A Recent History of Toad Hall

(with Special Commentary on its Exquisite Renovations)

I like saying 'eggs quizzit'

written by Toad, in the year 2017

Ice House Days

Comments by Teejay when Mr T was out

Icy incarceration! Despicable detention!
For a hundred years Toad Hall's illustrious
proprietor (yours truly) lay frozen in his own
ice house. He was chilled to insensibility by
scoundrelous weasels¹, while Toad Hall fell
into a lamentable decline around him.

He was frozen to sleep

Is this is a proper word?

Toad Arisen!

That's me, Mo and Ratty

Fortune favours the Toad! A band of brave children broke into the secret tunnels below Toad Hall. There they found Toad, lying amid the ice, ~~like an ancient king entombed upon the scene of his final battle.~~ *He was snoring and wearing a nightie* He awaited his moment to rise up and rejoin the fight against the Wildwood forces!

Once freed of his frozen prison, Toad immediately set about reclaiming Toad Hall from the clutches of the weasels. He bravely challenged the Chief Weasel to a motor race, which he won ~~with a magnificent display of courage and motoring skill.~~ *Because Mo's clever and Mr T is the worst driver EVER*

Chief Weasel   Mr Ripton   Weasels

Footnotes

[1] What rogues! What dastardly, conniving, mendacious, double-dealing twisters!

He's still grumpy with the Weasels

7

A Brave New World

and looking all
eggs quizzit

The Toad then set to work, restoring his home to its former glory. Toad Hall was soon completely renovated. But times, dear reader, move on—and the insightful and modern Toad must move with them! A new chapter has begun, marked by Toad's audacious new project to provide Toad Hall with the very best of Modern Conveniences[1].

I haven't seen any wizards. There are some squirrels. Are they squirrel wizards? Squizzards!

Technical Wizards

To this end Toad has contracted technical wizards to help him craft a masterpiece of modernity. It is his fondest hope that Toad Hall will henceforth stand as a beacon of beatitude and an example for the betterment of Animalkind.

Mrs Badger

Badge says that Toad Hall was already fine, and Animalkind would be better off without all the stupid gadgets

footnotes

[1] Many such innovations were designed by Toad himself and, he predicts, will soon become very silly indispensable additions to every household.

Mr T spent all weekend stuck to his anti-stoat glue-carpet

9

'**Are** you ready for this?' said Teejay, adjusting her helmet.

Ratty gripped his handlebars. 'I was born ready.'

'I wasn't,' said Mo.

Teejay sighed. 'Oh, come on, Mo. It's not like it's dangerous.'

'Hah. Remember the rope swing?'

There was a big pit in Toad Hall's lawn where Mo had fallen off the swing. Mr Toad had put up a sign that said *Caution: Mole Hole*.

'How could I know the rope would snap?'

11

said Teejay. 'Anyway this time we're on bikes, so it's different.'

The bikes were amazing. Mr Toad had bought them one each as a 'thank you' for getting Toad Hall back. They had electric motors that made them go very fast.

'Doesn't matter. I'm not racing.'

'OK, you can judge or something,' said Teejay. 'So here's the route, Rat: past Toad Hall, left at the Mystery Squirrel Van, over the

bridge, along the creek, jump over it, and the first to the back door wins.'

'Jump the creek?' said Mo. 'How?'

'Ratty made a ramp,' said Teejay, 'but we'll have to be going fast.'

'We'll use the motors,' said Ratty, 'like a turbo-boost!'

'Brilliant!' Teejay put her foot on the pedal. 'Now, are we talking or racing? Start us off, Mo!'

Ready, steady...

'All right. Ready . . . steady—'

'Go!' shouted Ratty, and sped off.

'Cheat!' Teejay pedalled after him.

Ratty zipped past Toad Hall's front door with Teejay just behind. His tail whisked past her face. She grabbed it, and dragged him back until they were level.

'Haha, gotcha! *Now* it's a race!'

They swung round the corner of the house, and there was the Mystery Squirrel Van. Teejay frowned at it. It was white, and on its side were the words, 'Squirrelwood Decorating ... We Have Designs on Your Home!'. Nobody

knew what the squirrels were doing in Toad Hall. Mr Toad might, but no one had seen him in weeks.

'Watch where you're going!' yelled Ratty.

'Oops!'

Teejay swerved, just missing the dustbins. She put her head down and cycled faster. They rattled over the bridge and on down the side of the creek, dodging trees. They skidded around the boathouse. And there in front of them was the ramp. Beyond it lay Toad Hall, the finishing line.

'Eat my dust!' yelled Teejay. She pushed the button, and the electric motor whined. Then her bike shot forwards.

Whhhoooosh!

'No, no!' yelled Teejay. 'Too fast, too fast!'

She grabbed the brakes, but too late. Her bike hit the ramp and bounced into the air. She flew over the creek and landed with a jolt that knocked her from the saddle. She fell off, right into a bush.

Crack, snap, rustle!

'Ouch,' said Teejay. 'Actually, big ouch.'

She climbed out, covered in scratches. Her leggings were torn and her jacket had a brand new rip in it.

'Oh nuts! Badge is going to kill me.'

Ms Badger always made Teejay promise to take care of her clothes. Somehow she never managed it.

NoOOO!

'I thought toads were good at jumping,' called Ratty from the other side.

'Very funny,' said Teejay. She looked around. 'Hey, where's my bike?'

Ratty's eyes widened. 'Oh no!'

Teejay's bike was still going, racing at top speed towards Toad Hall's back door.

'Stop!' she yelled. 'Stop, you stupid bike, you're going to—'

Crash!

The door slammed open. The handle fell off, and bits of broken lock tinkled to the ground.

'Ooh, nasty,' said Ratty. 'Mr Toad's only just finished the place, too.'

Toad Hall had been a ruin for a hundred years, but after all Mr Toad's rebuilding it looked as good as new—except, now, for the back door. Teejay watched as it swung in the breeze.

'Maybe we could put the handle back on? You know, so he doesn't notice.' Teejay looked at Ratty. 'Got any sticky tape?'

Ratty rolled his eyes. 'I don't think—'

Vrreeeeeeeee–eeeeee–eeee!

'What's that noise?' said Ratty.

'I don't know.' Teejay frowned at the door. 'But it's coming from inside the house.'

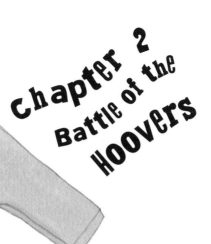

Chapter 2
Battle of the Hoovers

Vrreeeeeeeee-eeeeee-eeee!

'What are you doing?' It was Mr Toad's voice, yelling inside Toad Hall. 'Leave that alone!'

Vrreeeeeeeee-eeeeee-eeee!

Mo ran up, panting. 'Someone's shouting. Is everything all right?'

'I think Mr T's in trouble,' said Teejay. 'Rat, get round here.'

'On my way!'

Vrreeeeeeeee–eeeeee–eeee!

'Back, you brute!' cried Mr Toad. 'Get back or I'll take my stick to you!'

Vrreeeeeeeee–eeeeee–eeee!

'No! No! Not my trousers. Not my trousers!'

Vrreeeeeeeee–eeeeee–EEEEEEEEE!

Ratty cycled up, and jumped off his bike. 'I'm here, what's the plan?'

'We're going in to help, that's what,' said Teejay.

'But we're not allowed,' said Mo.

Mr Toad had told them not to come in until Toad Hall was finished. He wanted everything to be a surprise.

'This is different,' said Teejay. 'It's an emergency. Come on!'

They dashed through the door, heading for the noise.

–EEEEEEEEEE–EEEEEE–

'Let go! Let go, I tell you!' yelled Mr Toad.

–EEEEEEEEEE–EEEEEE–

'Let. Go. Now!'

21

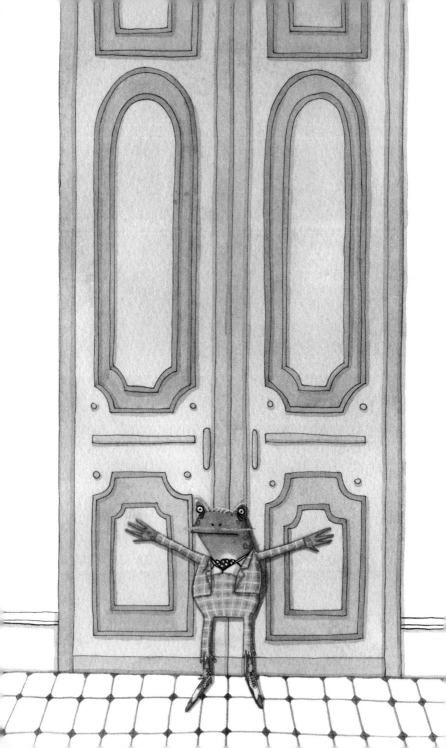

Clang!
'Ha ha! Take that!'
Clang! Slam!

VREEEEEEEEE–EEEEEE!

Teejay, Ratty, and Mo skidded down the corridor and into the main hall. And there was Mr Toad with his back against the ballroom doors, holding them closed. The bottoms of his trousers were ripped to tatters.

'Are you OK? What's going on?' shouted Teejay.

'They've gone berserk! I've shut them in the ballroom,' cried Mr Toad. He pointed to a cupboard. 'Quick, fetch brooms. I'll keep them back.'

Ratty grabbed two brooms and a mop. He threw one each to Teejay and Mo. They lined up, facing the doors.

VRRREEEEEEEEEEEE–vREEEEEEEEE!

23

Teejay gripped her mop. The noise was really loud.

'W-what's in there?' said Mo.

Mr Toad's face was grim. 'Hoovery things.'

'What?' said Ratty.

'No time to explain.' Mr Toad jumped back from the door. He grabbed a stout walking stick. 'We must do battle!'

VRRREEEEEEEEEEEE–VREEEEEEEEE!

'They sound angry,' said Ratty. 'Good thing we're wearing bike helmets.'

'Can't we leave them in there?' quavered Mo. 'You know, until they've calmed down?'

'I can't have a horde of hoovery whatsits rampaging round my ballroom,' said Mr Toad. 'We must show them what's what!' He lifted his walking stick above his head and cried, 'Are you with me?'

Ratty swallowed. Mo looked scared. But both of them nodded, and raised their brooms.

'We're with you,' said Teejay.

'Excellent fellows,' said Mr Toad. He took hold of the door handle. 'So here's the plan: we dash in there and let the blighters have it.'

'That's not a plan,' said Ratty, 'that's—'

Mr Toad yanked the door open.

VRRRREEEEEEEEEEEEEEEEEEEEE!

Two hoovers raced out and zipped across the hall.

'Brace yourselves!' cried Mr Toad.

The hoovers spun about, and rushed back towards them.

'Look out!' Teejay leapt aside.

The first hoover bashed into Mo's ankle.

'Argh!' Mo dropped his broom, hopping on one leg. Then the hoover knocked his other leg out from under him. Mo fell to the floor and the hoover buzzed around him, trying to suck up his jumper.

'It's malfunctioning,' Mo wailed. 'Get it off me!'

'Hang on, Mo, I'm coming!' yelled Teejay.

But the other hoover had caught her shoelaces.

28

VREEE–EEEEEEE!

Thwack! She hit it with her mop and it zoomed off.

'That's the spirit,' yelled Mr Toad. 'Give 'em some stick!'

Ratty shoved Mo's hoover back with his brush. Mo rolled to his feet, grabbed his own broom, and together they swept it away. Teejay chased after the other one.

'Haha! Just the ticket,' cried Mr Toad, bashing left and right with his walking stick. 'They've tangled with the wrong Toad! Herd the devils into the corner!'

They rounded the hoovers up and Teejay, Ratty, and Mo pinned them against the wall.

'Great,' Teejay panted. 'Mr T, can you switch them off?'

Mr Toad reached for the nearest hoover. It leapt forward with a loud **VRRREEE!** He snatched his hand away. 'Good gracious! A chap could lose his fingers.'

'So what do we do?' said Ratty. 'We can't

stand here for the rest of our lives.'

'I have an idea,' said Mo. His eyes glinted dangerously. 'I know just where to put them.'

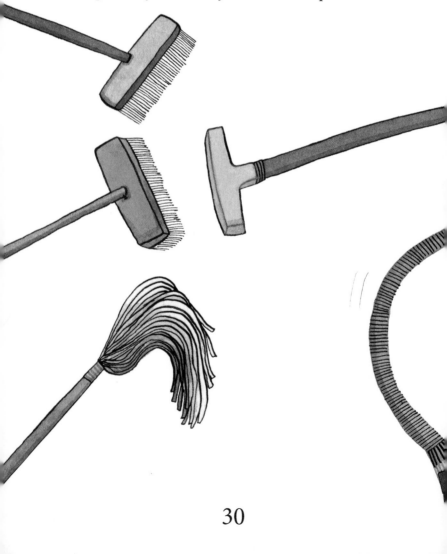

Chapter 3
Down the Hatch

Mo ran to the pantry and pulled open the trapdoor. Teejay, Ratty, and Mr Toad swept the hoovers towards it.

'Top notch plan, young Mole,' shouted Mr Toad over the noise. 'Let's see how these vacuum-louts enjoy the ice.'

The trapdoor led to Toad Hall's icehouse and a secret tunnel. Mr Toad didn't go down it any more, because the weasels had once trapped him in there.

Teejay swept the first hoover right to the edge of the hole. It struggled and waved its hose.

31

'Ooh, can I do it?' said Ratty. 'Can I, please?'

'Go for it, Rat,' said Teejay.

Ratty held his brush under his arm like a lance. He took a run up and—*clunk!* The hoover toppled over the edge.

Vvvvvrrreeeeeeeeeeeeeeeeeeeeeeeeeeee!

'Hoover jousting,' Ratty grinned.

'Fine fellow. Now permit me to dispatch the second,' said Mr Toad. He crouched like a golfer. He swung his walking stick.

'Fore!'
Clank!

Vvvvvrrreeeeeeeeeeeeeeeeeeeeeeeeeeee!

The second hoover disappeared into the darkness. Mo slammed the trapdoor, and sat on it. 'Phew,' he said. 'Good riddance.'

'We made a clean sweep of 'em,' said Mr Toad. 'Now, how about a rousing song of victory?'

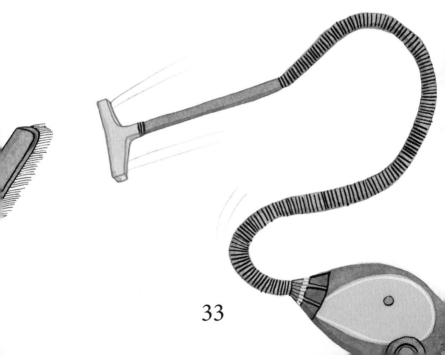

'No, I'm OK,' said Ratty, quickly. But Mr Toad had already started.

'The battle is done, two victorious Toads,
And Ratty and Mo, 'gainst our hoovery foes.
Their hoses thrashed wildly, but brooms
proved their match,
We swept to triumph, they went down
the hatch!'

He beamed at the children. 'Haha! Did you like it?'

'Very, um, rousing,' said Teejay. 'But where did the hoovers come from?'

'My Squirrelwood chaps found 'em for me,' said Mr Toad.

'Squirrelwood?' said Teejay. 'You mean from the Mystery Squirrel Van?'

'The very same,' said Mr Toad. 'But there's no mystery. I hired them to find me new gadgets. Just the chaps to kit out a modern home!'

'You don't *have* a modern home,' said Ratty.

'Well that shows what you know,' said

Mr Toad. 'I was hoping to keep this all as a surprise, but how would you like a little tour? I can show you what we've done with the old place.'

Teejay glanced at Ratty and Mo, who nodded. 'Definitely!'

'Good show. Follow me!'

Mr Toad ran to the kitchen. The fireplace and ovens were gone. Instead the room was filled with gleaming metal and shiny kitchen gadgets.

Mo made a squeaking noise. 'It's beautiful!'

'But there's nowhere to cook,' said Ratty.

'Cook? Pah! Who needs to cook?' said Mr Toad. 'These machines produce any food I desire.' He pointed at one with a huge, shiny nozzle. 'See this contraption? Makes fried eggs. Who wants one?'

'I do!' said Teejay.

'With you in two ticks!' Mr Toad shoved six eggs down a funnel in the top, and tapped a control pad. 'Settings, settings,' he muttered.

'Oil temperature optimal, egg-speed to eight
. . . and go!' He pushed a button then held a
plate under the machine's nozzle. Oil bubbled,
the machine whirred, and—

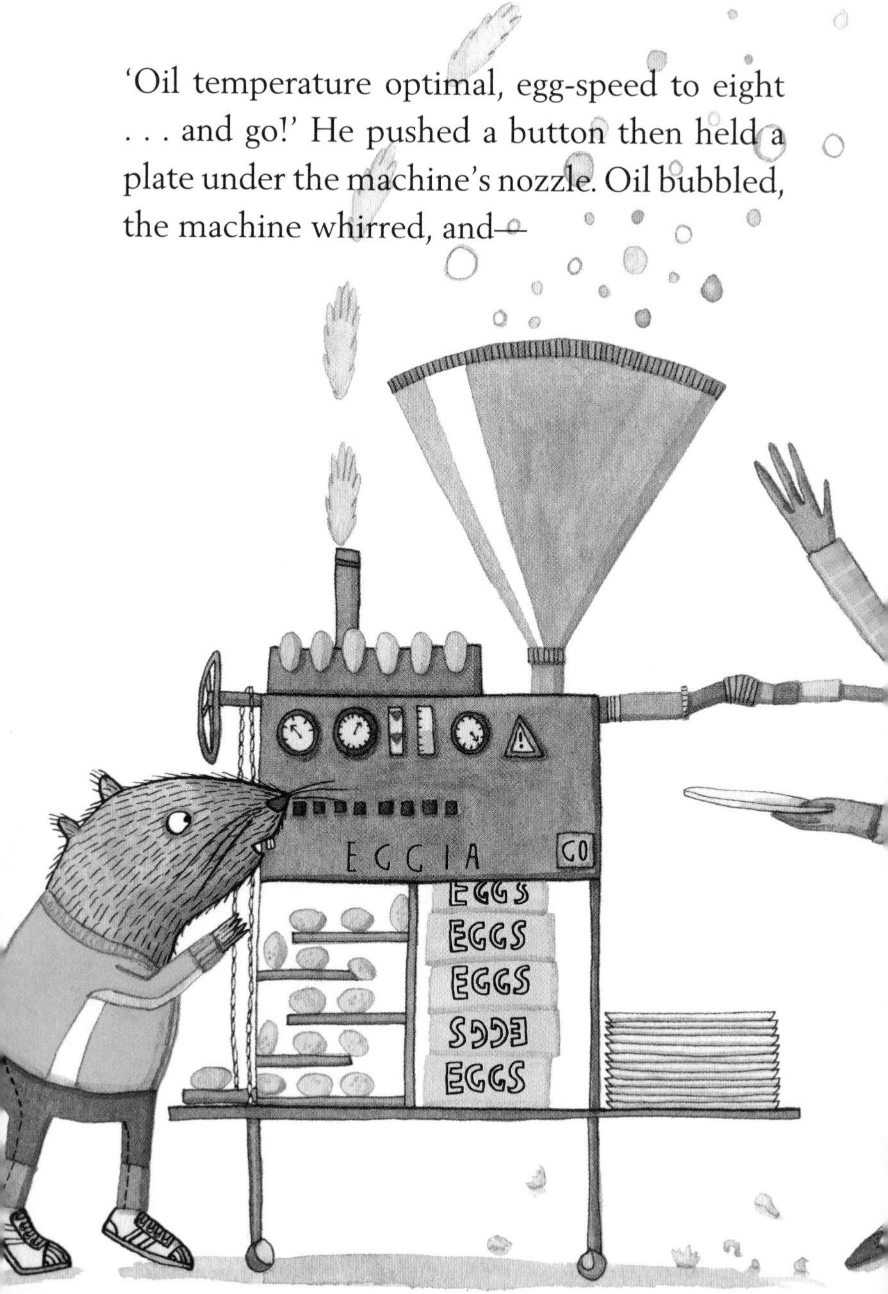

EGG1A   GO

EGGS
EGGS
EGGS
EGGS
EGGS

—Fffff-put.

A fried egg shot out. It bounced off the plate and hit the wall.

Fffff-put. Ffffff-put-put.

Three more eggs pinged off in different directions. Mr Toad waved his arms, and pressed all the buttons on the control pad.

The machine stopped with a groan. A final egg flopped out, and Mr Toad caught it on the plate.

'There you are! Marvellous, isn't it? I've nearly got the hang of it, too,' Mr Toad clapped Teejay on the shoulder. 'More to see, more to see!' he cried, and dashed from the room.

Chapter 4
Modern Marvels

Mr Toad ran to the main staircase.

'Here's my new motor car!'

A metal rail now ran up the old banister. On it was a seat shaped like a racing car. Mr Toad climbed on, legs dangling.

He winked at the children. 'Newfangled toad sensors,' he said. 'Watch this!'

He gripped the steering wheel and the car shot up the banister. It jerked to a stop at the top, dumping him on the carpet.

'Jolly little thing, isn't it?' said Mr Toad, dusting himself off. 'Brakes need a spot of work, though. Come on up, I'll show you the rest.'

Mr Toad strode into his bedroom. He clapped his hands and the curtains opened. He clapped again and the lights came on.

'Ooh!' said Mo.

'Clever, eh? Controlled by Dumb Pewter,' said Mr Toad.

'You mean "computer",' said Ratty.

'Yes, yes,' said Mr Toad. 'Ah, do you see this? Automatic pillow fluffer. Everyone should have one. Careful, there! Keep back from that.' He waved Ratty away from a machine that looked like it was made of scissors. 'That's my haircutting thingy—can't get it to stop.'

Teejay picked up an object. 'What does this do?'

'Personal hygiene,' said Mr Toad. 'It trims nose hair, tidies eyebrows, and cleans your armpits.'

'Oh.' Teejay put it back. Then she wiped her hand on her jumper.

Mr Toad pointed at a sofa. 'What do you think of my bath?'

'I think it's a sofa,' said Ratty.

'On the contrary.'

Mr Toad tapped a control screen. The sofa sank down into a hole in the floor. A tap popped out of the side and started filling the hole with water.

'Sofa-bath!' said Mr Toad. 'For the gentleman bather who values his comfort.' He grinned at them. 'Well, what do you think? Toad Hall looks good, doesn't it?'

'It looks . . . different,' said Ratty. 'But where's all your old stuff gone? You know, the tables and chairs and pictures and things?'

Mr Toad goggled at him. 'You mean to tell me that you're standing here, surrounded by

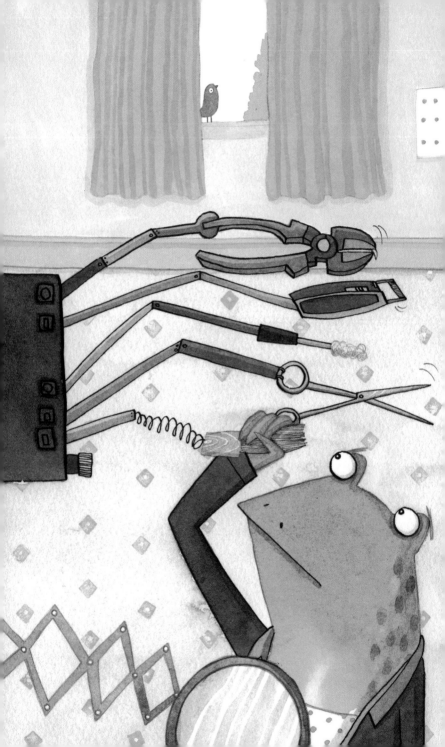

the most marvellous of modern masterpieces, and all you can think about is a load of silly, old-fashioned furniture?'

'But it was nice,' said Ratty. 'It—it just looked right, that's all.'

'My dear young Rat, you clearly are an animal of very little taste.' Mr Toad gave him a stern look. 'Anyhow, I gave all that tat to the Squirrelwood chaps. They're taking it away.'

'Where to?' said Teejay.

'Who cares? Out with the old, in with the new, that's my motto!'

Mo's eyes were shining. 'I think it's amazing,' he said. 'All of it. But where did you get the money?'

'An excellent Mole and a good question,' said Mr Toad. 'Quick, back to the pantry!'

They scampered after him as he raced down the back stairs. Hidden behind the tins on the pantry shelf was a cupboard. Mr Toad pulled it open. Inside was a rusty safe.

'What I'm about to show you is of the

utmost secrecy,' said Mr Toad. 'Nobody is ever to know. Agreed?'

They nodded.

'Very well.' Mr Toad took a key from his pocket and turned it. He grasped the safe's handle and pulled.

Chapter 5
Safe as Houses

'**Whoa!**' said Ratty. 'That's a lot of shiny things.'

Teejay stared. Stacks of gold coins and boxes of expensive jewellery filled the safe.

Mr Toad nodded. 'The Toad family fortune. It's been kept here ever since there were Toads in Toad Hall. Safe as houses!'

'But—but aren't you worried?' said Teejay.

'Worried? Whatever for?'

'What if the weasels break in?' said Mo.

'They wouldn't dare!' said Mr Toad.

'They've already done it,' said Ratty. 'Twice.

Wildwood Industrious would love to get their paws on that lot.'

'Which is why I ensure the doors are locked every night.' Mr Toad smiled. 'They may be old, but they're solid.'

Teejay glanced at Ratty. 'Right,' she said. 'Yes. About that, I -'

'After all, they've stood firm for centuries,' said Mr Toad.

'Mr Toad, I think you—'

'They're impregnable, unassailable, they're—' He paused, one finger in the air. 'I say . . . just out of curiosity, how did *you* all get in?'

The weasels!

'I broke the back door,' said Teejay. 'Sorry.'

'Broke it?' Mr Toad stared at her. 'How?'

'All I did was hit it with my bike. It just kind of . . . opened.'

Mr Toad went pale. 'Oh my good gracious!' He held his hands to his face. 'The weasels! All my money, all these beautiful things! What can I do, what can I do?'

Mr Toad stared around the pantry. His fingers twitched. 'Squirrels,' he muttered. 'Squirrels. Of course! Squirrels will help.'

He blinked at Teejay, Ratty, and Mo as if only just seeing them. 'Right. Good. Well, anyway, must get on. Time's ticking and I'm a busy Toad. Lots to do, that sort of thing.' He ushered them towards the front hall. 'Enough chit chat. Lovely to see you all, good day!'

He pushed them onto the doorstep and slammed the door. They heard his footsteps running back into the house.

'Well that was rude,' said Ratty.

'He's worried,' said Mo. 'If the Chief Weasel

49

found out about that money . . .'

'Yes, but how are the squirrels meant to help?' said Teejay.

'You can ask them,' said Ratty. 'They're over there.'

Two squirrels in overalls were carrying a table out of the back door. They threw it into the van and went back in the house. They returned with armfuls of chairs.

'Hey, that's Mr Toad's old furniture,' said Teejay. She raised her voice, 'Excuse me, where are you—'

The squirrels froze. Then they dropped the chairs and dashed into the house. They slammed the back door with a bang—right on one of their tails.

'Argh, no!' said Ratty. 'That has to hurt!'

The tail hung there, sticking out from the side of the door.

'Ooh, horrid!' Teejay

53

ran up, and shoved at the door.

'Don't worry, we'll get you free!'

But the door did not move.

'It's shut tight!' said Teejay.

'It can't be,' said Mo, 'you broke the lock.'

'Come on, then, help me!'

Ratty and Mo joined in. They all pushed together, but still the door would not budge.

'They're holding it shut,' said Mo.

'What? Why? If that was my tail I'd want it open really fast,' said Ratty. He picked up his tail and stroked it. 'Don't worry,' he whispered, 'I won't let it happen to you.'

They tried again. The door stayed tight closed. They knocked and hammered. No reply.

'This is really weird,' said Teejay.

Mo frowned. 'You know, those squirrels did look strange. A bit kind of . . . thin.'

'Right.' Teejay stopped pushing and picked up her bike. 'Something's going on and we're going to find out what it is. Can you fix my wheel, Rat?'

'Sure!' He pulled a spanner from his pocket, and set to work.

'Great.' Teejay pointed at the Mystery Squirrel Van. 'Because they'll have to leave soon, and when they do we're going to follow them.'

Chapter 6
Squirrel Stakeout

The Mystery Squirrel Van raced ahead of them. Teejay could just glimpse it through the hedge.

'There it is, go faster,' she cried.

Teejay's plan had worked perfectly. They had waited, hidden in Toad Hall's trees, for the van to leave. And now the chase was on. They pedalled furiously down the footpath, trying to keep up.

'It's no good,' Ratty gasped. 'It's going too fast!'

'Use the motors,' yelled Teejay. 'Ready?'

'Not again,' Mo whimpered.

'Just do it. Ready, steady, go!'

They pressed the buttons. Their bikes surged forwards.

'Wheee!' shouted Ratty.

'Eeek!' wailed Mo.

'Out of the way, out of the way!' Teejay yelled. People leapt off the path as the bikes flew past.

'Sorry!' shouted Mo back to them. He bumped over a hole, and nearly lost his grip. 'Argh, I hate this. Why can't we cycle on the road?'

'Because they'll see us, of course!' said Teejay.

'And Mum won't let me,' said Ratty. 'She says the road's too dangerous. Look out, Mo!'

Mo ducked as a branch whipped over his head. 'Too dangerous?' he shouted. 'How can it be worse than this?'

'Keep going,' shouted Teejay, 'they're getting away.'

'I don't care!'

'Look, there,' said Ratty. 'They're stopping. They're going in!'

The van turned through a gateway in a huge, brick wall.

Teejay skidded to a stop and jumped off her bike. Ratty and Mo pulled up behind her.

'That,' Mo panted, 'was the worst thing ever.'

Ratty grinned. 'You said that about Mr Toad's driving.'

'That was the worst thing ever too.'

'Shush!' Teejay hissed. 'Quick, get back against the wall.' They pressed themselves to the bricks. 'Look—look where we are!'

Above the gates a sign said:

WELCOME TO WILDWOOD INDUSTRIOUS

We ferret for your future

'We're at Wildwood!' Mo gasped. 'But why would the squirrels come here?'

'We can find out,' said Ratty. He pointed down the wall to where piles of old crates and bricks were stacked high. 'Fancy a climb?'

'Brilliant, Rat!' Teejay clambered to the top of the bricks. She peered over the wall. On the other side was a car park full of vans. The squirrels drove up and got out.

''Ere, Wes,' said the first squirrel, 'can you give me a hand with this? I'm really hot in here.'

'Right you are, Wilbur,' said the second.

He grabbed his friend's tail, and pulled.

Rrrrriiiiipp! The tail came clean off in his paws.

'Oh, yuck!'
said Teejay.
'What,
what's yuck?'
said Ratty.
'They're pulling
each other's tails off!'
'They're doing *what?*'

Ratty joined her up on the bricks.

The first squirrel threw the tail to the other. 'There you go,
matey.'

Then he reached
up and yanked off
his ears.

64

'That's nasty,' said Ratty. 'Mo, you should see this.'

Mo climbed up, carefully. He blinked. 'Something tells me those aren't real squirrels.'

The first not-a-squirrel reached into his mouth. He fiddled around then pulled his teeth out.

'That's better,' he said. 'Squirrel teeth make me talk funny.'

'Make you look funny too, Wes. Why do we have to dress like this anyway?'

'Don't be daft. If old Toady knew we were weasels he'd go bananas. Go on, call the others.'

'Weasels!' hissed Teejay. 'They're weasels in disguise.'

'Told you they were thin,' said Mo.

'They've been working in Toad Hall,' Ratty whispered. 'For weeks. That can't be good.'

Beep! Beep!

The van's horn echoed around Wildwood's car park. Then the not-squirrels flung open the van's back doors.

'What are they doing now?' said Teejay.

Mo pointed at Wildwood Industrious. 'Look!'

Weasels were pouring from the building, heading straight for the van.

LOT NO.	DESCRIPTION
87	4 x dining chairs
88	1 x dining table
89	6 vase
90	big oil painting - man in hat
91	green armchair
92	small oil painting - boat
93	6 x small plates
94	crystal glass bowl

A crowd of stoats and weasels gathered around, chattering excitedly.

'Ladies and gentlestoats,' cried Wesley, 'we are proud to present the latest furniture, fresh from The House of Toad.'

Teejay heard chuckles from the crowd.

'There's some lovely bits too,' said Wilbur. 'See this beautiful old dining table and chairs?' He lowered his voice. 'This very table was once used by the old chief weasel himself.'

'It's proper vintage,' said Wesley. 'Best quality. So who'll start the bidding?'

Hands shot up among the weasels.

'Oh no! They're selling all Mr T's stuff,' Teejay hissed. 'We've got to stop them!'

'How?' said Ratty. 'There's loads of them.'

'And anyway, Mr Toad gave it all away,' said Mo.

'But they're weasels! What if he wants it back?' said Teejay.

'Then he shouldn't have chucked it out,' said Ratty.

They watched stoats and weasels staggering away under Mr Toad's old tables, chairs, and wardrobes. Soon only Wilbur and Wesley were left. A mobile phone rang, and Wilbur answered it. He nodded, listening.

'Who do you think it is?' said Mo.

'Shh, I'm trying to listen,' Teejay whispered.

'. . . yes, yes, of course, sir,' said Wilbur. 'You can rely on us. We'll be right there.'

He put the phone back in his pocket. 'Back into the squirrel outfit, matey. That was old Toady.' Wilbur grinned. 'He says he wants

security to keep weasels out.'

'If only he knew,' chuckled Wesley. 'Sounds like Project Lock 'n Toad is go!'

'That's right, Wes. The Executive will be properly chuffed. I'd like to see old Toady's face when—'

Slam! Wilbur shut the van doors.

'What are they saying?' said Mo. 'I can't hear what they're saying. Can either of you hear anything?'

'No, we can't,' said Ratty, 'mainly because of you.'

'Quiet!' Teejay hissed.

'—lockdown before he knows what's happening,' said Wilbur. 'Anyway, come on, let's get going.'

'Oh no, we missed their plan!' said Teejay.

'I don't like the sound of "Lock 'n Toad",' said Mo.

'Me neither. What are we going to do?'

'I'll tell you what you're going to do,' said a voice behind them. Teejay spun around. At the bottom of the crates stood Ms Badger, arms crossed. She did not look pleased.

'I think you're in trouble,' whispered Ratty to Teejay.

'What you're going to do,' continued Ms Badger, 'is tell me why I've just spent two hours looking for you.'

Teejay swallowed. 'Two hours?'

'That's right. You didn't come home. But apparently lots of other people knew where

73

TOAD HALL IN LOCKDOWN

you were.'

'Really?' said Mo. 'How?'

Ms Badger's frown deepened. 'Do the words "three maniacs on bicycles" mean anything to you? You nearly ran over half the town!'

'Badge, I'm really sorry,' said Teejay, 'but we had to catch the squirrels—'

'Squirrels?' said Ms Badger. 'Squirrels? What have squirrels got to do with anything?'

'They weren't really squirrels,' said Ratty.

'They were weasels,' said Mo, 'but they looked like squirrels.'

'That's right, they were squirrel-weasels,' said Teejay.

'Squeasels,' said Ratty.

'Squeasels with gadgets—'

'—and they fooled Mr Toad—'

'—but shut a tail in the door—'

'—and then they drove here—'

'—and pulled their teeth out—'

'—then beeped for more weasels—'

'—and sold all his chairs—'

'Stop, stop,' Ms Badger put a paw to her head. 'I'm getting a headache. You're not making any sense.'

From behind the wall they heard van doors slam. An engine started.

'Oh no,' said Ratty, 'the van's coming back!'

'Quick, Squeasels!' hissed Teejay. 'Hide!'

They grabbed Ms Badger and dragged her behind a hedge. They got down just as the van

roared past and away down the road.

Teejay jumped to her feet. 'See, Badge? They're off to Toad Hall!' Teejay was bouncing on the spot. 'We need to follow them, we—'

Teejay stopped dead. Ms Badger stood up from behind the bush. Her hair was caked in mud. Twigs and leaves clung to her coat. She glowered.

'The only place any of you are going,' she

growled, 'is home. Understood?'

'But—'

'Home!' shouted Ms Badger. 'Right now! You can explain yourselves when we're there.' She took a breath. 'And believe me, the explanation had better be amazingly good.'

Chapter 8

The TechnoToad KG-1908

'**Please**, Badge. Please drive faster.'

'I don't drive fast,' said Ms Badger. 'I'm not Mr Toad. Anyway, we're nearly there. Five more minutes won't matter.'

Ms Badger had listened to their story, then promised to take them to Toad Hall in the morning. Teejay had spent the whole night awake, imagining everything the weasels could be up to.

'Here we are,' said Ms Badger. 'Toad Hall.'

But the iron gates were shut. Ms Badger stopped the car.

STO A S

'That's odd. Mr Toad never closes the gates.'

Ratty tapped Teejay on the shoulder. 'There's the Mystery Squirrel Van,' he hissed. The van came down the drive towards them. It stopped on the other side of the gates, blocking the way. Written on the side was: 'Squirrelwood Security. We'll Pick Your Locks for You!'

'It's a different van,' said Mo.

'But the same weasels,' said Teejay.

'Squeasels,' said Ratty.

'Weasels, Squeasels,' Ms Badger's eyes narrowed, 'whatever they are, they're in my way.' She leaned out of the window. 'Excuse me, I'm trying to get past!'

The squirrels did not move. They stared at Ms Badger.

'You three go and find Mr Toad,' Ms Badger ordered. 'I'm going to give these Squeasels a talking to.'

Teejay, Ratty, and Mo jumped from the car. They slipped through the gate and ran for Toad Hall.

'Look,' cried Teejay. 'There's Mr T!'

Mr Toad was standing in front of Toad Hall, hands on his hips. He grinned when he spotted them.

'What ho!' he called. 'Fancy seeing you fellows here. Marvellous morning, isn't it?'

'Is everything all right?' shouted Teejay. 'What did the weasels do?'

'Weasels?' said Mr Toad. 'What weasels? Who could be worried about weasels on a day like this?' He winked at Teejay. 'Not me, that's for certain. Not now I've had my new security installed.'

'Wait, what?' said Ratty. 'You let them give you security?'

'Certainly did! They even replaced that silly, rusty old safe.' Mr Toad marched up to his front door and gave it a pat. 'Those squirrel chaps worked all night. The place is locked tight and stoat-proof. Do you like it?'

Teejay stared at Toad Hall. The old wooden front door was gone, replaced by smooth, shiny metal. The windows were new too, with thick, blueish glass.

'Wow,' said Teejay, 'I don't know. It looks a bit . . .'

'Ugly?' Mo suggested.

'That's the word,' said Ratty. 'It doesn't even look like Toad Hall any more.'

But Mr Toad was running his hands over the

door. 'It's a miracle,' he whispered. 'A modern marvel of weasel-resistant magnificence.'

'But how do you get in?' said Mo. 'There's no handle.'

'Ah!' Mr Toad's eyes twinkled. He pulled a black object out of his pocket. 'Behold the TechnoToad KG-1908!'

Mo peered at it. 'That's a TV controller.'

'And someone's glued straps to it,' said Ratty. 'Weird.'

'Don't be silly,' scoffed Mr Toad. 'The squirrels explained everything. This device unlocks the most advanced anti-stoat defences in the world. Just watch this!'

Mr Toad strapped the controller to his arm.

'I utter the secret words—in my most mellifluous tone—and the door obeys.' He pointed at the door. 'Open sesame!'

Nothing happened.

'Oh, silly old Toad, I forgot to press the buttons.' Mr Toad tapped at the controller then pointed again. 'Open sesame!'

Nothing.

'I said "open sesame"!' Mr Toad pointed harder, waggling his finger. 'Come on, sesame, open up!' He waved his arm up and down, pushing all the buttons. 'I don't understand it. This is what the squirrels did.'

'Mr T,' said Teejay, slowly, 'I'm not sure the squirrels gave you proper security.'

'Stuff and nonsense,' said Mr Toad, 'fine fellows the pair of them! I'm an infallible judge of character.'

'What does that mean?' whispered Teejay.

'It means he's a twit,' said Ratty.

'Just teething troubles,' said Mr Toad, tapping

the controller. 'After all it's very advanced stuff. All controlled by Dumb Pewter!'

'Ah, so there's a computer, is there?' Mo's eyes gleamed. He took off his rucksack and pulled out a laptop. He walked up to Toad Hall, tapping at the screen.

Mr Toad pointed and shouted. But whatever he did the door stayed shut.

'I know the problem!' he announced. 'The mechanism's jammed. Nothing a hearty shove won't put right.'

'I wouldn't do that,' said Mo.

But too late. Mr Toad took a run up and—

Thump!

'Oooh!' he staggered away, rubbing his shoulder.

A light above the door began to flash.

'Oh dear,' said Mo, 'it's going into lockdown.'

'Lockdown? That sounds bad,' said Ratty.

A siren rang out.

Awwwwooooffaa! Awwwwooooffaa!

'Yes,' said Mo, shouting over the din. 'It's definitely bad.'

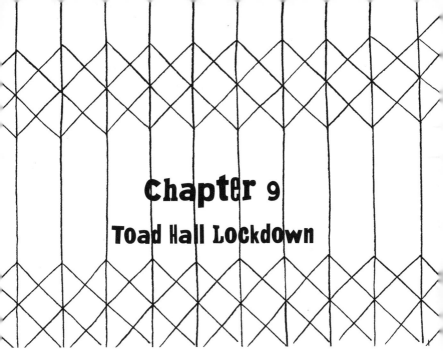

chapter 9
Toad Hall Lockdown

Awwwooooggaa! Awwwwooooggaa

Intrusion attempt detected! Lockdown initiated.

'Argh, loud!' yelled Teejay. She scuttled back from the house. Ratty and Mo ran after her, paws over their ears.

Mr Toad was still by the door, waving the controller at it. 'Quiet! I command you to be quiet!'

Awwwwooooggaa!

Lockdown commencing in twenty seconds!

'I'm Toad of Toad Hall! I'm the holder of the TechnoToad!'

Awwwwoooooggaa!

Lockdown commencing in fifteen seconds!

owWWWWW!

'What's wrong with you, you wretched thing?' Mr Toad kicked the door as hard as he could.

Clunk!

'Owwwww!' He hopped away, clutching his foot.

Awwwwooooggaa!

Lockdown commencing in ten seconds!

Mr Toad stared at Mo. 'How do I stop it?'

'You need a computer override code,' Mo shouted. 'Four numbers. Have you got one?'

Mr Toad pulled a piece of paper from his pocket. He read it. 'No, nothing here!'

Ratty put his head in his paws. 'The weasels locked him out, didn't they?'

Awwwwooooggaa!

Lockdown commencing in five seconds!

'I'll show you,' yelled Mr Toad. 'There's

more than one way into Toad Hall!'

He grabbed the window and heaved. Then he climbed onto the ledge and hammered on the glass with his fists.

'Let me in! You're testing the Toad's tolerance!'

Clear the building. Lockdown commencing!

Clang!

A steel shutter slammed down across the door.

Clang! Clang! Clang!

Shutters crashed over the windows. The last one squashed Mr Toad flat against the window ledge.

'Ouf!' Mr Toad wiggled his arms and legs. 'I'm trapped. Let me free!'

Lockdown complete. Have a nice day!

'Mo, do something,' said Teejay.

'I can't. It's password-protected,' said Mo.

'Instructions,' gasped Mr Toad. He waved his piece of paper. 'Lockdown instructions.'

Teejay took the paper from Mr Toad's hand. It said:

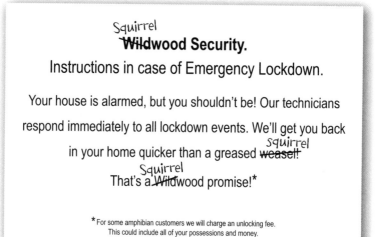

Squirrel
~~Wildwood~~ Security.

Instructions in case of Emergency Lockdown.

Your house is alarmed, but you shouldn't be! Our technicians respond immediately to all lockdown events. We'll get you back in your home quicker than a greased ~~weasel!~~ *squirrel*

That's a ~~Wildwood~~ *Squirrel* promise!*

*For some amphibian customers we will charge an unlocking fee.
This could include all of your possessions and money.

'There's good news and bad news,' said Teejay. 'The good news is that the weasels are coming to unlock Toad Hall.'

'And the bad news?' said Mo.

Teejay handed him the paper.

Mo read it. 'They can't do that!'

'I bet they're going to try,' said Ratty.

A car raced down the drive, Ms Badger behind the wheel. She stopped and jumped out.   'I heard an alarm,' she said. 'Are you all OK?'

'We're fine, Badge,' said Teejay. 'But Mr T's stuck.'

'A terrible indignity,' cried Mr Toad. 'When I see those squirrels, I'll give them a piece of my mind!'

'You don't have much to spare,' muttered Ratty.

'Badge, how did you get through the gates?' said Teejay.

'The Squeasels just opened them,' Ms Badger frowned, 'but I don't know why.'

'I think I do,' said Ratty. 'Here they come!'

The Squirrelwood Security van drove up and stopped in front of Toad Hall. Teejay could see Wesley and Wilbur through the van's window. They had taken off their squirrel outfits.

'Weasels!' Mr Toad gasped. 'The fiends, they've kidnapped my squirrels!'

Ratty sighed. 'Will somebody please just tell him?'

'There never were any squirrels, Mr T,' said Teejay. 'It was weasels in disguise.'

'And now they've brought friends,' cried Mo. 'Look!'

Three more vans raced down the drive and stopped in front of the house. Then a large, black car rolled into view. It pulled up right next to Mr Toad. Its door swung open.

'**Hurk hurk**,' laughed a voice. 'Why, bless my soul. Look, Mr Ripton, it's Mr Toad!'

Chapter 10

Teejay grabbed Ratty's arm. 'It's the Chief Weasel,' she hissed.

'And he's brought his legal weasel,' said Mo.

'Y-You!' gasped Mr Toad.

The Chief Weasel stepped from his car, followed by a thin weasel in a grey suit. 'That's right, Toady. Me.'

'What are you doing here, weasel?' Mr Toad waggled a finger under the Chief Weasel's nose. 'Get off my property this moment. Go on, buzz off, or I'll call the law!'

'My dear Mr Toad, you misunderstand.'

99

The Chief Weasel gave him a nasty smile. 'We simply came to help our valued customer. Isn't that right, Mr Ripton?'

The grey weasel nodded.

'Customer?' Mr Toad blinked. 'What are you talking about?'

Mr Ripton opened his briefcase and handed the Chief Weasel some papers.

'Mr Toad, could you confirm that this is your signature?' said the Chief Weasel.

Mr Toad's eyes widened. 'But that's the contract I signed with those squirrelly security chaps!'

'I think that's a "yes", Mr Ripton.' The Chief Weasel smirked. 'You see, Mr Toad, some contracts have lots of very small words. You should always read them.' He held up the paper. 'These words say that Squirrelwood Security is owned by Wildwood Industrious—which is owned by me.'

Mr Toad goggled at him. 'You mean—'

'I'm in charge of your security,' finished the Chief Weasel. 'That's right. Now, why don't you tell me what the trouble is?'

Mr Toad's mouth opened and shut. 'I . . . Well, I—' Mr Toad swallowed. 'I'll tell you what the trouble is. I can't get into my house, that's what!' He raised his chin. 'So open it up immediately.'

'Of course,' said the Chief Weasel, 'but first there's the small matter of the unlocking fee. We charge it to any customer called "Mr Toad".

It says so right here, in these tiny weeny words right at the bottom.'

Ms Badger stepped forwards, glaring at the Chief Weasel. She put her hand on her hips. 'How much is the fee?'

The Chief Weasel gave her a toothy smile. 'Just everything Mr Toad owns and all his money, that's all. Hurk, hurk,'

'So that's your game, is it? Steal my family fortune, eh?' Mr Toad folded his arms. 'Well you won't have a penny.'

'Then good luck getting into Toad Hall, Mr Toad. Our security is the best there is. It's proof against invasion for ten years.'

'Ten years,' gasped Mr Toad.

'Exactly. So I hope you like the outside of your house,' said the Chief Weasel. 'Because you'll be looking at it for a long time. Hurk hurk.'

He started to get back into his car.

'Wait,' said Mr Toad. 'You can't just leave me stuck like this. Let me free!'

'Not without the fee,' snarled the Chief Weasel.

Mr Ripton opened his briefcase. He pulled out a form and a pen.

'It's the unlocking form,' said the Chief Weasel. 'Sign it, Mr Toad, and you'll get your house back. It's better than being trapped under a window.'

Mr Toad stared at the Chief Weasel. His lip quivered. 'Y-you're a monster,' he said.

'Tut tut, Mr Toad. I'm a simple business-weasel, that's all,' said the Chief Weasel.

'I have to give you everything, don't I?' A tear rolled down Mr Toad's cheek. 'I don't have a choice,' he sniffed. He took the pen and signed the paper. 'There,' he said. 'I've signed your beastly form. Now let me into my home!'

'Poor Mr Toad,' said the Chief Weasel. 'Tears falling like summer rain. **Hurk**, **hurk**. Mr Ripton, would you kindly do the honours?'

Mr Ripton nodded, then walked past Mo to the door. (Mo was busily working at his laptop.)

He pulled a keypad from his pocket and tapped in a code.

Defences deactivated! Please enjoy your house.

'Such a useful device, Mr Ripton's keypad,' said the Chief Weasel. 'It holds the master code to all Wildwood's security. Even to your brand new safe, Mr Toad. If only you'd known. **Hurk, hurk.**' The shutters rose. The door clicked and swung open. Mr Toad tumbled to the ground. He glared up at the Chief Weasel.

'You'll pay for this!' he said.

'No, Mr Toad, *you'll* pay for this.'

The Chief Weasel and Mr Ripton got in the car. It roared off down the drive. Then the vans opened and weasels poured out, heading for Toad Hall.

'They're going in,' said Teejay. 'They're

going to take all his money!'

Mr Toad uttered a terrible cry. He bounded to his feet.

'Weasel invasion!' he yelled. 'I'm under attack! The Toad shall never surrender!'

He dashed for Toad Hall, barging stoats and weasels aside. And then he disappeared into the house.

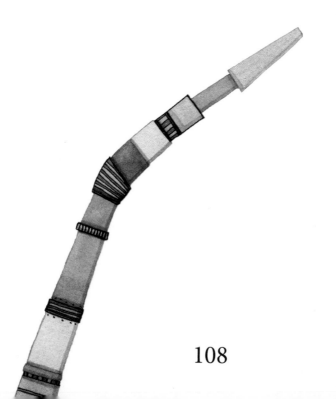

Chapter 11
Eggs of Vengeance

Mo ran up to Teejay and Ratty. 'I've got it, I've got it,' he said. 'I know how to get back at the weasels, I—' Mo blinked. 'Where's Mr Toad gone?'

'Back inside,' said Ratty.

'Oh no!' said Mo. 'Get him out. We have to go to Wildwood!'

'Right.' Teejay sprinted after Mr Toad. A weasel at the door made a grab for her, but she ducked, and ran into Toad Hall. Stoats and ferrets were everywhere, taking Mr Toad's gadgets and chairs, and carrying them out of the house. Teejay found Mr Toad in the kitchen, stacking furniture across the doorway.

'Toad Junior, you came!' he cried. 'You came to support your dear old Toady!'

'What? Well, sort of, but—'

'Such loyalty, such bravery.' Mr Toad grabbed her hand, and shook it. 'Together we stand, the last bastions against the weasel tide!'

'Mr T, Mo has a plan. We should go!'

'It's too late for plans.' Mr Toad wiped a tear from his eye. He raised his chin. 'My safe is unlocked, my fortune undefended! But we shall fight to our last breaths. Not one measly weasel shall penetrate this pantry!'

Mr Toad grasped the fried egg machine. He wheeled it to the

door, nozzle facing outwards.

'Ha ha! I'd like to see the weasel who can make his way past this little beauty,' said Mr Toad. 'How many eggs do we have?'

'Um, ten boxes, but—'

'That's sixty shots!' cried Mr Toad. 'We'll make them count.' He dragged up a chair, and stood on it. He gripped the machine's handles and tapped the buttons on its control pad.

'There, I've turned it up to eleven,' said Mr Toad. 'Maximum egg-speed!'

A hissing, bubbling sound rose from the machine.

Teejay tried again. 'Mr Toad, we don't have to. We can—'

'Surrender? Never! Quickly now, here they come. Load the first box!' commanded Mr Toad.

'Aye, aye, sir!' Teejay grabbed the first box of eggs and tipped them into the funnel at the top. The machine started to shake and shudder.

'She's ready to fire,' said Mr Toad. 'Just time

for my battle song!

*'The Wildwooders came down like a wolf
on the Toad
And their cohorts were grinning, their
tactics were bold;
And their numbers were mighty, like
stars on the sea,
But Toad's fried eggs were ready, and
soon to fly free!*

'Steady now,' he said, 'here they come!'

'Don't shoot until you see the whites of
their eyes,' said Teejay. She grinned. 'I heard
that in a film.'

Mr Toad's jaw set. 'I'll shoot, and they'll see
the whites of my eggs.'

A weasel ran down the corridor towards the
kitchen. It was Wilbur. Mr Toad took aim. And
his finger stabbed the control pad.

FFFFFFFFFFffff–PUT.

A fried egg splatted on Wilbur's jumper.

Yolk splashed his whiskers.

'Argh!' shouted Wilbur, clutching his chest. 'I'm hit, I'm hit!'

He staggered back, colliding with Wesley and two stoats that were running after him.

FFFFFFFFFfff-PuT. FFFFFFFFFfff-PuT-PuT.

Eggs hurtled down the corridor. They bounced off walls, and smacked into stoats. Attackers slipped on grease and tumbled to the floor.

FFFFFFFFFfff-PuT-PuT-PuT. FFFFFFFFFfff-PuT.

Mr Toad smothered them in eggs. 'Load, load!' he yelled.

Teejay grabbed more boxes and emptied them into the funnel.

The machine whined and gurgled. Eggs whizzed and weasels stumbled.

115

'We're scrambling them!' shouted Mr Toad. 'It's a stoat omelette! Haha, hot eggs of vengeance! I'll sprottle the lot of you!'

But Wilbur had climbed to his feet. He licked his whiskers. His eyes narrowed.

'It's eggs,' he yelled. He dragged Wesley to his feet. 'Old Toady's firing food! Come on, let's get 'im!'

chapter 12

Look what You've Done to Toad Hall

Eggs pelted but the weasels kept coming.

'No, no!' said Mr Toad. 'Stay back, stay back.'

Wesley and Wilbur marched up and unplugged the machine. The stoats grabbed Mr Toad and Teejay and carried them from the kitchen.

'Unhand me, you scoundrels!' cried Mr Toad.

'Hey, leave me alone,' said Teejay. 'I can walk!'

The stoats dropped them on their bottoms

119

on the front doorstep. Then they disappeared back inside, chuckling.

Teejay climbed to her feet. 'Meanies,' she said 'Are you OK, Mr T?'

Mr Toad shook his head, sadly. He sat against Toad Hall's wall, his legs in front of him. He pointed a trembling finger at the weasels who were loading their vans with his gadgets and money.

'Look what they're doing,' he whispered. 'Taking everything I have.' He held up the unlocking contract. 'And worst of all, it's *legal!*' he howled.

'It's your own fault,' said Ms Badger. 'All that silly stuff and security. You didn't need any of it. I mean just look at what you've done to Toad Hall.'

Mr Toad stared up at the security windows, and the black metal door. He sniffed. 'You're right. Oh, of course you're right.' He laid his cheek against the wall, and stroked the bricks. 'You poor old thing, what did I do to you?' he whispered. 'I'll make you right again, I promise.' He paused. 'But I *can't* make you right. I don't have any money!'

And Mr Toad collapsed to the ground, sobbing.

'Chin up, Mr Toad,' said Ms Badger. 'At least you've still got your house. And Mo has a plan. So there's hope!'

Mr Toad raised his head. He climbed to his feet, and very humbly said, 'Dear lady, is there truly hope? I'd be ever so grateful.'

'There is,' said Ms Badger, 'but it's a lot more than you deserve.'

'I know, I know. I've been a very silly Toad indeed. And I'm truly sorry.' He clasped his hands together. He gave her a smile. 'But please, dear Ms Badger, please do what you can, and I'll be a good Toad and put Toad Hall all back how it should be. Please?'

'You promise? You'll make Toad Hall exactly how it was? And no more gadgets?'

'Yes, yes, absolutely,' said Mr Toad.

Ms Badger held out her paw. Mr Toad took it. They shook, solemnly.

'It's a deal,' she said. 'And now everybody run to my car. Quickly now!'

Mr Toad's eyes widened. 'My dear lady, what are we going to do?'

'What you're going to do is get in the car and keep your hands away from the steering wheel,' said Ms Badger. 'What I'm going to do is drive. Very, very fast.'

Chapter 13
The Coming of Wildwood's
Uppance

Ms Badger's car skidded around the final bend and roared through the gates of Wildwood Industrious. She kept the car at full speed until the last possible moment, then screeched to a stop outside the offices. Only then did Teejay let go of the seat.

'Oh my gosh,' she said.

'I feel sick.' Ratty put a paw to his head. 'I'll just sit here until everything stops moving. How's Mo?'

Mo was still hunched over his laptop, typing.

'Didn't even notice,' said Teejay. 'I never

thought you could drive like that, Badge!'

'Neither did I,' said Ms Badger. Her eyes were shining. 'I was good, though, wasn't I?'

'I can only say "**poop-poop**",' said Mr Toad.

'Do you mean it?' said Ms Badger.

'I certainly do.'

Ms Badger looked pleased. Then she raised her voice. 'OK, everybody out,' she ordered.

124

'The vans will be here any moment! Remember the plan?'

'Indeed,' Mr Toad nodded. 'Wildwood's comeuppance is at hand!'

'Good, but remember, I don't want Mo in any trouble. The weasels have to think this is your idea.'

'Madam, you have my word.'

'How about you, Mo? All set?' said Ms Badger.

Mo looked up from his laptop, and smiled. 'Oh yes,' he said. 'All set.'

'Then get to work,' said Ms Badger.

Mo and Mr Toad walked up to the front door of Wildwood Industrious. Mo held up his laptop and frowned at the screen.

'OK,' he muttered, 'excellent signal . . . good connection . . .' He tapped his laptop. '. . . password . . . and we're in.'

'You have control of their security?' whispered Mr Toad.

Mo grinned. 'Like the Chief Weasel said, Wildwood have a master code for all of their computers.' He patted his laptop. 'I stole it when they unlocked Toad Hall.'

Two security ferrets came to the door, blocking the way. 'You there,' shouted one, 'toad and mole. What are you doing here?'

Mr Toad walked straight up to him. 'Excuse me, my fine sir,' he said, 'could you kindly inform me whether the Chief Weasel might be in residence?'

'He's in, but that's none of your business. Now what are you doing here?'

Mr Toad held up the TechnoToad KG-1908. 'I came to test your security.' He pointed the controller at the door. 'Close sesame!' he shouted.

Mo tapped his laptop.

AWWWWOOOOOGGGAAAA!

AWWWWOOOOOGGGAAAA!

Clang! Bang! Clank! Clunk!

Doors slammed all around the building. Their locks clicked shut. Shutters crashed down, covering the windows. The main gate closed, just as the first van turned down the drive. In seconds Wildwood Industrious was sealed tight. The two ferrets hammered on the glass front door. But they could not get out.

'Well done, that mole!' said Mr Toad. 'Are

you sure they're stuck?'

'Yes, I've changed the passcode and everything.'

Mr Toad gazed at Wildwood Industrious. He stared at the queue of vans at the gate. 'Well, that's all marvellous!' He rubbed his hands together. 'And now the talented Toad shall mitigate this mess through the masterful misuse of mystifying mustelid misdirection.'

'What did he say?' asked Teejay.

'He's going to fool the weasels,' whispered Ms Badger.

'Ooh,' said Teejay. 'This I want to see.'

Executive Suite

Acquisitions and Ext... tio...

Weasel Resources

Accounts and Creative Fina...

Sales (Legitimate / Inventive)

Chapter 14

Toad Foolery

Mr Toad pressed the intercom next to the door.

'Good day, Toad here. I wish to speak with your Chief Weasel.'

The ferrets stared at him through the glass. Then they ran back deeper into the building. Soon the Chief Weasel appeared, with Mr Ripton behind him. He pressed the intercom on the other side. 'Toady!' he snarled. 'What have you done?'

Mr Toad held up the controller. 'I was merely testing my TechnoToad KG-1908.' He winked

TOAD HALL IN LOCKDOWN

at Teejay and Mo. 'It didn't work at Toad Hall, so I thought, "Toady, old boy, I wonder if those squirrels might have given you the wrong gizmo?" So I came here and tried it out.'

'What?' snarled the Chief Weasel. 'Are you trying to tell me that you've taken over Wildwood with that . . . thing?'

'Well, I must have.' Mr Toad gave the Chief Weasel an innocent smile. 'I pointed it at the building and said the magic word, and then all your alarms went off.'

'Don't be ridiculous,' said the Chief Weasel. 'It's a television controller. It's useless. Any fool can see that.'

'But I don't understand,' said Mr Toad, frowning. 'If it's useless then it couldn't unlock Toad Hall, could it? So you shouldn't have taken my money.'

Mr Ripton's eyes widened. He tapped the Chief Weasel on the shoulder and whispered in his ear. The Chief Weasel froze. Then his scowl deepened.

'Oh, very clever, Toady. Very good,' said the Chief Weasel. 'Mr Ripton says that device works perfectly. It's your fault you got locked out, and you're not getting your money back.'

'Well that's that, then.' Mr Toad turned to Ms Badger. 'Dear lady, children, it's time to go. We shall leave these gentlemen to it.'

'Wait, what about us?' shouted the Chief Weasel. 'Open this door! I have a building full of stoats and weasels!'

'Well, I'm very sorry,' said Mr Toad, 'but you see my problem. If this device is right for Toad Hall then it can't unlock Wildwood Industrious. But if you accidentally gave me the device for Wildwood, then it's your fault I couldn't get into Toad Hall, isn't it?' He grinned, and waved the Techno Toad KG-1908. 'Either way, if I unlock your building I want all my money back.'

'Not a chance, Toady,' spat the Chief Weasel. 'You just wait till I'm out. I'll make your life a misery.'

'Temper, temper,' Mr Toad grinned. 'But you'll have plenty of time to calm down. Your security is guaranteed for ten years, I hear.'

Mr Ripton did more urgent whispering. The Chief Weasel's paws clenched. He glared at his legal weasel, who shrugged.

'Right,' growled the Chief Weasel. 'Mr Ripton says that Squirrelwood Security might have accidentally given you the wrong unlocking device.'

'And?' said Mr Toad, enjoying himself.

The Chief Weasel ground his teeth. 'And so we'll give you back half the unlocking fee.'

'Back in the car, everyone,' called Mr Toad. 'The weasel's unreasonable.'

'No, wait! We'll give it all back. I promise.'

'What a splendid chap you are,' said Mr Toad. 'I can see why they made you Executive. Now put that down in writing, if you please.'

Mr Ripton pulled out a form. The Chief Weasel snatched it off him, and signed it. Then Mr Ripton opened the letterbox and slid the paper out.

Mr Toad read the form, then tucked it in his pocket. 'Thank goodness, my money's safe! And so are all of my lovely gadgets.'

'Ahem.' Ms Badger folded her arms.

Mr Toad caught her eye. 'But of course I shall sell the gadgets to pay for the repairs to Toad Hall.'

'What a good idea,' said Ms Badger.

Mr Toad put a hand on Mo's shoulder. 'Young mole, you've saved my bacon. Your Dumb-Pewter wizardry has foiled the weasels. I am in your debt, and in debt to you all once again.' He bowed to Mo, and then to Teejay, Ratty, and Ms Badger. 'And now,' he said, 'I rather think we should put an end to all this muddlesome modern meddling.'

Mr Toad strapped the TechnoToad to his arm. He stood in front of Wildwood Industrious. He pointed at the Chief Weasel's scowling face.

'Right-eo, Mo,' whispered Mr Toad, 'are you ready to release the weasels?'

Mo quietly opened his laptop. He held a finger poised above it.

'Oh yes,' said Mo with a smile. 'I was born ready.'

chapter 15

underground Insecurity

The last of the white vans pulled out of Toad Hall's drive. The Chief Weasel, spitting in fury, had ordered Mr Toad's old safe to be returned, and filled with his money. And the old doors and windows had all been put back. Even the back door was mended, with a new lock.

'There you go, Mr T,' said Teejay. 'Everything's how it should be.'

'At last,' said Mr Toad. 'But the place looks rather empty. I don't see why we couldn't make the weasels give my furniture back.'

139

'Because they bought it fair and square,' said Ms Badger. 'It's your fault for giving it away in the first place.'

'You could always try to buy it off them,' said Teejay.

'I suppose so.' Mr Toad sighed. 'Such a lot of nonsense over some piffling security. But I've learned my lesson. You won't catch me worrying about weasel invasions again.'

'It's funny you should say that,' said Ratty, 'because I just remembered about the secret passage.'

'Oh,' Teejay blinked. 'Of course! We could have used the tunnel to get in.'

'And there's an entrance just there, where I fell through the lawn,' said Mo.

Mr Toad smiled, ruefully. 'Do you know what? In all that fuss I clean forgot about it. What a silly old Toad, eh?' Then he froze. 'But-but I say, that passage comes out in my pantry.'

'Yep,' said Ratty, 'right next to your safe.'

But Mr Toad was not listening. He was

sprinting across the lawn towards the Mole Hole.

'My safe's not safe!' he cried. 'I'm betunneled and insecure!'

He jumped down the hole and disappeared.

'You shouldn't have reminded him,' Ms Badger groaned. 'You've set him off again.'

'But it's a security risk,' said Teejay.

'Actually I'm not so sure,' said Mo.

'Really?' Ratty blinked. 'Why not?'

A muffled noise rose from the earth beneath their feet.

Vrreeeeeeeeeee–eeeeeee–EEEEEEEE!

'Argh! Vacuum attack!' cried Mr Toad below them. 'Get away from me, you despicable hoovers!'

vRRREEEEEEEEEEEE–vREEEEEEEEE–vRREEEEEEEEE!

They heard two loud thumps and a scuttling noise. Then Mr Toad burst from the Mole Hole, scrambling for safety. He was covered in mud and his sleeves and trousers were shredded. He stared around him, wild eyed.

'They—they were down there, waiting!' he gibbered. 'Waiting in the tunnel.'

'I don't understand,' said Ms Badger. 'What were down there?'

'The hoovery whatsits! They're down there I tell you!'

Teejay started laughing. She couldn't help it. 'Well they would be, wouldn't they?' she said. 'We pushed them through the pantry hatch, remember?'

Ms Badger looked alarmed. 'Are we safe? Can these things get out?'

Ratty shook his head. 'The tunnel's pretty steep. I think they're stuck in there for good.'

Mr Toad stared at him. 'Stuck there, you say? For good?' A slow smile spread across his face. 'And how long do we think those hoovery thingies might last? You know, before they run out of juice?'

'Well, if they're on standby, then maybe

twenty years,' said Mo.

'Twenty years, eh?' Mr Toad rubbed his hands together. 'Well that's splendid. Looks like I've managed to install the best tunnel security a chap can afford! Now,' he said. 'I was thinking of a picnic down by the boathouse. Just a little something to say thank you. What do you all say?'

Teejay glanced at Ms Badger, Ratty, and Mo. They nodded eagerly.

'I think that sounds lovely, Mr T,' she said.

'Top hole! I'll get cleaned up, you chaps fetch the basket.' Mr Toad started walking towards Toad Hall. 'Down by the river. Just the place to forget all this modern malarkey. Cool water and lazy days. Ducks, swans, reeds, willows, that sort of thing.' He paused, one finger in the air. 'And boats. Great big, beautiful boats.' He smiled, dreamily. 'Boats, now there's a thought.'

'Oh no,' Ratty whispered, 'please not boats.'

'Why? What can go wrong on a boat?' said Mo.

'I don't know,' Teejay grinned, 'but I've got a feeling we're going to find out.'

Fin
(Sploosh)

The Wind in the Willows

The River Thames

Kenneth Grahame is the author of *The Wind in the Willows,* the book which has introduced generations of children to Mr Toad and his friends. Kenneth Grahame was born in 1859 and spent much of his childhood exploring the idyllic countryside along the banks of the River Thames and discovering its wildlife.

A water vole

Kenneth Grahame

After leaving school he began a career in the Bank of England. He married Elspeth Thomson in 1899 and they had a son, Alastair. When Alastair was about four years old, Kenneth Grahame began telling him bedtime stories that were to form the beginnings of *The Wind in the Willows*. The book was published in 1908 and has been loved by readers ever since.

The Real Toad Hall?

Mapledurham House, close to the River Thames, is mentioned in the Domesday Book of 1086, although much of the house that stands today was built in the 16th and 17th centuries. The house is about 20 miles from the village of Cookham Dean, where Kenneth Grahame spent part of his childhood. Perhaps this grand house, with grounds sweeping down to the water, inspired Kenneth Grahame's descriptions of Toad Hall? Or was it another riverside property—there are other contenders—that might have been the real life 'Toad Hall'?

Mapledurham House

A note from Tom Moorhouse

Writing the second book of Mr Toad's exploits, *Toad Hall in Lockdown*, was tricky and wonderful. *A Race for Toad Hall*,

the first book, was great to write because I had brand new characters to create, and an old favourite—Mr Toad himself—to re-introduce to readers. It was fun to have them all meeting for the first time. In the second book, though, everyone already knew each other. So the tricky bit was making sure that readers who had missed the first book could understand what was happening. But mainly it was just wonderful to be back with Teejay, Ratty, and Mo (and the long-suffering Ms Badger), and to invent all those daft gadgets and silly situations that can only happen around the irrepressible Toad . . . !

A note from Holly Swain

Starting work on *Toad Hall in Lockdown* was like visiting old friends. Having already illustrated *A Race for Toad Hall*, the first book in *The New Adventures of Mr Toad* series, I knew who the characters were and what they looked like. Among all the familiar faces it was great fun to  draw lots of baddies—the weasels! I always start work on the pictures in pencil, drawing very roughly at first, and then redraw until I am happy with them. When I start to paint I use a dip pen (a bit like a fountain pen), watercolour paints, and coloured pencils. I absolutely loved making the pictures for this book, I hope you enjoyed it!

If you'd like to read the original story, we have these editions available.

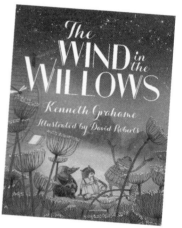